*"Look — what unity! How all the parts correspond
to the whole! What beauty there is in the buildings,
what taste and, overall, what variety, deriving
from the mix of water and edifices"*

Konstantin Batiushkov. 1817

S · A · I · N · T
PETERSBURG

P-2 PUBLISHERS

Introduced by Abram Raskin
Translated from the Russian by Paul Williams (introduction) and Valery Fateyev (captions)
Designed by Dmitry Trofimov
Photographs by Valentin Baranovsky, Leonid Bogdanov, Pavel Demidov, Konstantin Doka, Natalia Doka, Vladimir
Dorokhov, Sergei Falin, Pavel Ivanov, Grigory Khatin, Arthur Kirakozov, Pavel Kirillov, Pavel Kuzmichev, Vladimir
Melnikov, Victor Savik, Georgy Shablovsky, Oleg Trubsky, Victor Vasilyev, Vasily Vorontsov and Victor Yeremeyev
Edited by Maria Lyzhenkova
Art editor Nikolai Kutovoi
Managing editor Nina Grishina

ISBN 5-900530-12-4

It was long ago noted that the name of a place in many ways reflects and even predetermines its fate. In this light, the choice made for the maritime capital by its founder and spiritual father, Tsar Peter the Great, was a highly significant one. In the period immediately after the foundation of a six-bastion fortress on Zayachy (Hare) Island on 16 (27 New Style) May 1703 — the Orthodox feast of the Holy Trinity — Peter styled the new Russian settlement in letters and documents in a variety of ways. He was never in any doubt in whose honour the new city on the River Neva should be named — his heavenly patron, the apostle Peter. But the question of the language in which to convey the concept of a city — the native Russian suffix *-grad*, the Greek *-polis* or the German *-burg* — was not settled immediately. For a brief time Peter's documents employed the form *Petropolis*. Then that was succeeded by another *Piterburg*, incorporating a Dutch-sounding pronunciation of the apostle's name. Finally, though, the Tsar settled on another variant — *Sankt-Peterburg*.

This name was made up of three elements: Sankt (from the Latin *sanctus*); Peter (the German version of the name, which means *rock* in Greek; close enough to the Russian to be readily understood) and the German *-burg*. Thus the fine-sounding name of the young capital (anglicized as Saint Petersburg) might be said to have combined within it the cultures of the Ancient World and contemporary Europe as well as Christianity. It did not take long, however, for a popular, purely Russian variant to appear — *Petrograd*, which remained in frequent use, and from 1914 to 1924 had official status.

The complex name given to this maritime "paradise" expressed its royal founder's intention to turn the city into a European and even world centre of trade, science and culture, in which Russia would naturally play the leading role.

For Peter himself, the creation of a capital on the Baltic was the realization of an age-old dream, a successful end to the efforts of his predecessors on the Muscovite throne. That motive, implanted in the Tsar's mind by Providence, endowed him with superhuman energy, wilful determination and daring which at times went beyond all normal bounds.

When Peter founded and constructed St Petersburg, he acted not only as a statesman and military strategist, but also as an inspired artist. The city was his creation and in it he revealed himself with exceptional clarity as a distinctively Russian genius, capable of comprehensive vision and tremendous dash in bringing an unprecedented concept into being.

The idea that only Peter I was a powerful enough ruler to establish a city on the low-lying, marshy, frequently flooded lands in the mouth of the Neva is expressed in an old Finnish legend. It says that many tried to do so, but their buildings were swallowed up by the quagmire; only the hero Peter managed to overcome its black bottomlessness. He forged a city out of copper, held it in his hands and set it above the Neva on an invisible, but unshakeable spiritual foundation infused with a Faith that was tougher than rock.

In the immense St Petersburg approaching its three-hundredth anniversary, one can distinctly make out the construction dating back to Peter's time. First and foremost, it is the Peter and Paul Fortress and its cathedral, which is the successor to a wooden church founded on 29 June 1703 on the day of the apostles Peter and Paul. Other reminders of Peter's city are the building of the Twelve Collegia, the Kunstkammer (the first scientific museum and library), the tiny wooden house built for the Tsar on the right bank of the Neva, the Summer Palace and Gardens on the left bank. Peter ordered the construction of the Admiralty Shipyard with its tower crowned by a golden ship, the laying out of the "Neva Perspective Road" (Nevsky Prospekt), the foundation of a commercial port, the digging of canals and the establishment of factories.

Success in the war against the Swedes made the new city increasingly important. In 1712 it became the capital of the Muscovite state, which in 1721 turned into the Russian Empire. Almost everything we think of in the appearance, layout and even individual details of St Petersburg has its roots in Peter's time, in the Tsar's ideas, which were turned into architectural reality mainly by Domenico Trezzini.

A dominant role in the formation of St Petersburg's "spiritual aura", its stirring shapes and silhouettes, was played by the construction of churches. In 1709 the St Sampson Cathedral, dedicated to the great victory of Poltava, was founded. Later Peter established the Alexander Nevsky Monastery, the St Isaac's and Kazan Cathedrals. The first churches of other Christian denominations also appeared. In the next two hundred years St Petersburg became a place of true religious tolerance. The cityscape includes not only the golden tops of Orthodox churches, but also the domes and spires of Catholic and Lutheran churches, the dome of the synagogue, the dome and minarets of the mosque and even a Buddhist temple. They give their blessing and protection to St Petersburg, as it were, through a shared prayer recorded in stone.

At present more than fifty Orthodox places of worship are functioning in the city, including ten cathedrals. There are six Evangelical-Lutheran churches, two Roman Catholic ones and the same number of Armenian-Gregorian, a Buddhist temple, a congregational mosque and a choral synagogue.

St Petersburg and Kronstadt, its outpost in the Gulf of Finland, immediately became and have remained the capital of the Russian navy, the stronghold of its sea-going forces, the source and strength behind its most brilliant victories.

A foretaste of St Petersburg's significance in Russian naval history was the successful boarding by guards of two Swedish warships in the mouth of the Neva on 7 May 1703. From that time onwards, sailing frigates, and later ironclad vessels, became an inseparable part of the city — all flying the naval flag, a blue St Andrew's cross on a white ground, devised by Peter.

In the following centuries, the maritime capital Peter founded grew in step with the general changes in aesthetic tastes and each period left its mark on the city's appearance with artistically superb works of architecture, sculpture and design. Each of these stylistic layers reflects in many ways the particular qualities of a given reign. Yet throughout all its history we can observe a wonderful, mysterious phenomenon: Peter's far-sighted undertaking drew geniuses in the spheres of architecture, sculpture and other arts, inspiring them to greater heights of creation for the sake of the tremendous idea called St Petersburg.

The reign of Empress Anna, daughter of Peter's half-brother Ivan, in the years 1730–40 saw a continuation and completion of the construction work begun under the first Russian Emperor. The regularity of Peter's time acquired a stricter precision. The territory of the city was divided into five: the Admiralty, Petrograd, Vyborg, Liteiny and Vasilyevsky Island districts. This determined the direction of subsequent construction. The "trident" of roads fanning out from the Admiralty — Nevsky Prospekt, Voznesensky Prospekt and Gorokhovaya Street — was fully established. A number of major roads were laid out which continue to play an important role in the city's traffic system today (Sadovaya, Kolomenskaya, Razyezzhaya, Zvenigorodskaya and Preobrazhenskaya (Marat) Streets, Vladimirsky and Zagorodny Prospekts). All this reinforced and intensified the typical St Petersburg feeling of streets dynamically "unrolling" one into another. The most prominent and prudent architect of this decade was Piotr Yeropkin.

The mid-eighteenth-century reign of Peter's daughter Elizabeth was marked by the appearance in St Petersburg and the surrounding countryside of huge, monumental palaces with rich carved and moulded decoration. Even the relatively small buildings of this period stand out for the elegance and sculptural quality typical of the Baroque. It was in that style that the architect Bartolomeo Francesco Rastrelli enriched St Petersburg with his inimitably perfect and eloquent creations. Among the edifices built to his designs were the Winter Palace, palaces for the Vorontsovs, Stroganovs and Shuvalovs, and the inspired delight of the Smolny Convent ensemble in which golden domes seem to sing alleluia in an angel chorus around the central cathedral. The refrain is taken up by Savva Chevakinsky's St Nicholas Cathedral and its bell-tower, reflected in the water of the Griboyedov Canal.

In the 1760s, a new style, founded on the study of the art of Ancient Greece and Rome, became dominant in all spheres of Russian culture. Classicism was encouraged at the highest level — by Catherine II, Alexander I and Nicholas I. Over the course of some seventy years, it gave St Petersburg the "austere and elegant appearance" which so delighted Pushkin. Sounding out of harmony within the Classical St Petersburg and complementing each other, there are, however, other individual, clearly expressed themes full of a humanist spirit.

The reign of Catherine II, covering most of the second half of the eighteenth century, introduced symbols of flourishing art, science and industry into St Petersburg's architecture. That description certainly applies to the works of the great Giacomo Quarenghi — the Hermitage Theatre, the Academy of Sciences, the Smolny Institute and the State Bank. They are complemented by those of Jean-Baptiste Vallin de la Mothe — the Academy of Arts (with Alexander Kokorinov), the Great Gostiny Dvor, the Small Hermitage and the New Holland warehouse complex, and Yury Velten — the Large Hermitage. The stamp of brilliance also marked other buildings of the period: Antonio Rinaldi's Marble Palace and Ivan Starov's Taurida Palace.

The brief reign of the Romantic Emperor Paul I was illuminated by the flash of Vasily Bazhenov's genius.

His brilliant design for the Mikhailovsky (Engineers') Castle was somewhat modified in the course of construction by Vincenzo Brenna. Other survivals from Paul's time are the monument to Suvorov and the Rumiantsev Obelisk.

The monumental forms of edifices which took their scale from the Winter Palace were set off and enhanced by the granite embankments and bridges built in this period. The rivers and canals became architectural features incorporated into the ensembles along their banks.

In the architectural chronicle of St Petersburg, the reign of Alexander I, which exactly coincided with the first quarter of the nineteenth century, stands out for the brilliant works of Andrei Voronikhin (the Kazan Cathedral and Mining Institute), Andreyan Zakharov (the Admiralty) and Thomas de Thomon (the Exchange, Rostral columns and associated embankments). They were echoed by the Horse Guards' Riding-School (Quarenghi), the barracks of the Pavlovsky Guards Regiment (Vasily Stasov) and the Lobanov-Rostovsky mansion (Auguste Montferrand). These buildings from the first decades of the nineteenth century express with precision the greatness and indomitable spirit of St Petersburg and Russia as a whole, those qualities which made it possible to defeat Napoleon's tremendous invasion. The glory and triumph of the war years, 1812−15, inspired artists for decades to come. In architecture this was reflected in the emergence of the *Empire* style, a variety of Classicism which drew on the forms and images found in the art of Imperial Rome.

In this period, features betokening imperial and military grandeur became especially prominent in St Petersburg. They include the Moscow and Narva Triumphal Arches and, most striking of all, the brilliant creations of Carlo Rossi — the building of the General Staff and ministries on Palace Square, incorporating a triumphal arch, the Senate and Synod buildings, also linked by a triumphal arch, the Mikhailovsky Palace, the Alexandrinsky Theatre and the Public Library. The ideas of statehood and martial glory fused with high spirituality were expounded in the Trinity and Transfiguration Cathedrals (the former for the Izmailovsky regiment; the latter for all the guards) by Vasily Stasov. The culmination of this tendency came in the works of Montferrand — the Alexander Column (1834) and the Cathedral of St Isaac of Dalmatia (1819−53).

After almost a century of dominating tastes, Classicism waned and gave way to a whole spectrum of stylistic tendencies drawing on the art of all peoples and periods.

The expansion of St Petersburg's architectural palette had already begun in the second half of Nicholas I's reign. It continued with particular intensity through the reigns of Alexander II, Alexander III and Nicholas II, right up to the fall of the monarchy. The construction of this period was decisively influenced by the beginnings of a town-planning culture and an inherited understanding of the city as a single living, artistic organism. Erudition, a sense of scale and individual style enabled Andrei Stakenschneider to insert into the existing cityscape such imposing buildings as the Mariinsky Palace (for Grand Duchess Maria Nikolayevna), the palace of Grand Duke Nikolai Nikolayevich (the Palace of Labour) and the Beloselsky-Belozersky Palace. An important place in the city centre ensemble was taken by Konstantin Thon's terminal for the railway line to Moscow. The early-twentieth-century trends of Neo-Classicism, Neo-Renaissance and Art Moderne are splendidly represented in St Petersburg. Here Fiodor Lidval revealed his great talent in the Azov-Don Bank and a number of residential buildings. No less significant and characteristic of their period are Pavel Siuzor's building for the Singer sewing-machine company (now the House of Books), Alexander Gogen's mansion for the prima ballerina Mathilda Kschessinska, Gavriil Baranovsky's trading house for the Yeliseyev brothers and Andrei Belogrud's "house with towers".

The architectural chronicle of St Petersburg up to the early twentieth century contains a whole host of names — architects, engineers, sculptors and artists — together with the roll of their works. Each of them represents a vital detail, feature, colour or image in that great collective whole that is St Petersburg. That whole must also include individual buildings, ensembles and extensive new districts which have appeared since the 1920s.

The architectural projects of the 1920s and early 1930s clearly display the stylistic devices of Constructivism. They were followed by buildings which used the Classical system of orders and decorative motifs. Still, the most significant feature of the creation of new districts in the Soviet period was the preservation of St Petersburg's town-planning traditions and the architectural masterpieces of the past, many of which were damaged during the 1941—44 siege and restored in the first post-war decades.

St Petersburg is a record of past ages — reigns, historical events and achievements, an anthology of masterpieces by brilliant and outstanding architects, and a sort of text-book of architectural styles available to everyone.

St Petersburg is a city of rivers and canals, and hence a city of bridges (more than 400), many of which are known around the world for their original design and decoration.

St Petersburg is a city of splendid parks and gardens laid out in the eighteenth and nineteenth centuries. Among them are the regular Summer Gardens from Peter's time, the Taurida Garden — an example of the landscape style of the 1760s, and the park from the first quarter of the nineteenth century on Yelagin Island which overlooks the Gulf of Finland. It is washed by arms of the Neva and enriched by mirror ponds set among magnificent trees and shrubs.

St Petersburg is a city of monumental and decorative sculpture. The most dominant works commemorate Peter I, Catherine II, Nicholas I and Alexander III; the military commanders Suvorov, Barclay de Tolly and Kutuzov; the scholar and scientist Lomonosov; the poets Pushkin and Nekrasov; the composers Glinka and Rimsky-Korsakov. Busts pay tribute to Lermontov, Mayakovsky, Tchaikovsky, Gogol, Quarenghi and many other citizens of St Petersburg and Russia who brought glory to the country.

It might also be said that in St Petersburg sculpture hovers above the city. Think of the angel above the SS Peter and Paul Cathedral, the angels, Evangelists and saints on St Isaac's Cathedral, the figures of ancient warriors, commanders and others on and around the grand entrance to the Admiralty. Chariots of Victory dash across the sky above the Narva Triumphal Arch and the General Staff building. Bas-reliefs, masks of various kinds, symbolic emblems and decorative motifs adorn the facades of many buildings.

In all the facets of the gemstone that is St Petersburg, one detects the indivisible unity of Russian and European culture, a lively interaction resulting in enrichment on both sides. This fusion is the precious quality of St Petersburg as one of the cornerstones of the "common European house".

At the same time the whole history of the city demonstrates that St Petersburg, founded by Peter in a burst of creativity, was, as well as being the product of rational considerations, from the first a work of art. With time the new capital became a true synthetic masterpiece with a distinctive atmosphere, embodying and retaining the secret of Kitezhgrad, the Russian fairy-tale city, infused with the light of Truth and Beauty.

*"...chief river of the northern land,
the Neva bright and grand"*

Piotr Viazemsky

In the course of human history, the names of rivers have often come to stand for civilizations, peoples and cities. It is enough to mention the Nile, the Euphrates or the Tiber to conjure up images of Ancient Egypt, Assyria and Babylon or Ancient Rome. You have only to say "the Volga" anywhere in the world and people know you are talking about Russia. In the same way the Neva has become identified with St Petersburg.

The Neva is the mother, nursemaid and governess of one of Russia's, and the world's, great cities. The glory of the Russian imperial capital extended to what, according to geographers and hydrologers, is the smallest of Europe's major rivers. It flows 74 kilometres from Lake Ladoga to the Gulf of Finland, only 28 of them within the city. Yet the shape of the Neva, the size and power of its waters have shaped the character of St Petersburg.

It was the Neva which determined the very appearance of St Petersburg as a port city, a centre for shipbuilding and a connecting link between vast continental Russia and the countries of Western Europe. Rulers, times, morals and styles all changed, a way of social and political life that had lasted for centuries was swept away, but the Neva still remains the main artery of the city.

From the earliest years of the city's existence, the banks of the Neva were reinforced and decorated. In the second half of the eighteenth century, the authorities began to clad them in granite. Throughout the nineteenth and twentieth centuries, a concern for the beauty of the Neva expressed itself in the construction of more and more granite embankments, landing-stages and jetties, decorative sculptures, vases and openwork railings. Eight mighty drawbridges, exceptional in terms of construction and decoration, were thrown across the main course of the river.

The main squares of the city either lie directly on the Neva or are spatially tied to it: Labour (Annunciation), Decembrists' (Senate), Palace and Suvorov Squares as well as the Field of Mars.

Soaring above the river are the spire of the SS Peter and Paul Cathedral surmounted by the city's guardian-angel (122.5 metres) and the Admiralty spire with its sailing-ship under the Russian naval flag of St Andrew (72.6 metres). These twin golden landmarks glistening in the sun are echoed by the domes and crosses of churches — St Isaac's (103.9 metres), the Winter Palace church, the Saviour-on-the-Spilt-Blood, the Prince Vladimir Cathedral, the church spire of the Mikhailovsky (Engineers') Castle and the domes of the Smolny Convent (93.08 metres).

St Petersburg's role as the Russian maritime capital is symbolized in the decoration of the buildings along the river's banks: depictions of Neptune, the ancient god of the sea with a trident in his hand, tritons, dolphins, and other lesser Greek and Roman deities associated with navigation, shipbuilding and trade.

For the inhabitants of St Petersburg, the Neva is a mirror of their life. At each new encounter with the river, one's gaze is drawn again to admire its majestic, unfading beauty.

The Large Neva. The Lt Schmidt (Annunciation or Nikolayevsky) Bridge.
1843–50. Engineer Stanislaw Kierbedz, architect Alexander Briullov

University Embankment. The landing-stage with sphynxes near the Academy of Arts.
1832–34. Architect Konstantin Thon

**University Embankment
Obelisk: To Rumiantsev's Victories.**
*1799. Architect Vincenzo Brenna,
sculptor Pierre Louis Agie*

**University Embankment
The Academy of Arts.**
*1764–88. Architects Jean-Baptiste Vallin de la Mothe
and Alexander Kokorinov*

University Embankment. The Menshikov Palace.
1710–27. Architects Giovanni Fontana and Georg Schädel

The Menshikov Palace. Barbara's Chamber

The Menshikov Palace. The Walnut Room (Alexander Menshikov's Study)

Decembrists' (Senate or Peter's) Square

**Equestrian monument to Peter the Great
(The Bronze Horseman).**
*1766–82. Sculptor Etienne Maurice Falconet
(with Marie-Anne Callot and Fiodor Gordeyev),
architect Yury Velten*

**Decembrists' Square
The Senate and Synod building.**
1829–34. Architect Carlo Rossi

St Isaac's Cathedral.
*1818–58. Architect Auguste Montferrand,
sculptor Ivan Vitali*

*St Isaac's Cathedral. **The central nave***
Stained-glass window in the chancel: Christ.
1840. Artist M. Einmiller

*St Isaac's Cathedral. **The main iconostasis***

**St Isaac's Cathedral. The drum
of the main dome. The ceiling painting.**
*Painter Karl Briullov. Statues of angels. Sculptors
Ivan Vitali, Robert Zaleman, Alexander Beliayev*

**St Isaac's Cathedral
The drum colonnade of the main dome**

The Admiralty
The tower with triumphal gates.
1806–23. Architect Adrian Zakharov,
sculptors Feodosy Shchedrin and Ivan Terebenev

Admiralty Embankment
The Eastern Pavilion of the Admiralty
1820–24. Architect Louis Charlemagne,
engineer Andrei Gotman, sculptor Ivan Prokofyev

The Admiralty. The Conference Hall

View of University Embankment from the left bank of the Neva
The main building of the Academy of Sciences.
1783–89. Architect Giacomo Quarenghi.
The Kunstkammer.
Architects Georg Johann Mattarnovi, Nikolai Gerbel and Gaetano Chiaveri

The Spit of Vasilyevsky Island. Festive illumination

**The Spit of Vasilyevsky Island
The base of the northern Rostral
Column.**
*1807–10. Architect Jean Thomas de
Thomon*
Allegorical statue: The Neva.
Sculptor I. Camberlain
Decorative rostra: Mermaids.
1810. Unknown sculptor

Ensemble on the Spit of Vasilyevsky Island.
1806–16. Architect Jean Thomas de Thomon

The Peter and Paul Fortress. *1705–34. Architect Domenico Trezzini*
The Naryshkin Bastion. The Trubetskoi Bastion

The SS Peter and Paul Cathedral
The western front.
1712–33. Architect Domenico Trezzini.
The Boat House. *1761–62. Architect Alexander Vist*

The Peter and Paul Fortress
View from Palace Embankment

The Peter and Paul Fortress. The Peter Gate.
1714–18. Architect Domenico Trezzini,
sculptor Hans Konrad Ossner

The Peter and Paul Cathedral
The central nave. The iconostasis.
1722–26. Architect Ivan Zarudny

The Peter and Paul Cathedral
The iconostasis. Icons: Queen Bathsheba
and Prince Alexander Nevsky.
Mid-18th century. A. Pospelov and F. Protopopov

View on the Palace Square

Palace Embankment. The southern and western fronts of the Winter Palace.
1754–62. Architect Bartolomeo Francesco Rastrelli

The Winter Palace
Decorative sculpture on the balustrade.
1754–62. After drawings by Bartolomeo Francesco Rastrelli, sculptor Iosif Boumchen. 1896–01. Sculptor Mikhail Popov

**The Winter Palace
The Main (Jordan) Staircase.**
1762. Architect Bartolomeo Francesco
Rastrelli; 1831. Architect Vasily Stasov

**The Small Hermitage
The Pavilion Hall.**
1858. Architect Andrei
Stakenschneider

**The Winter Palace
The Peter the Great
(Small Throne) Room.**
1833. Architect Auguste Montferrand;
1839. Architect Vasily Stasov

On the next pages:

**The New Hermitage
The Snyders Room
(Room of Flemish Painting)**

**The New Hermitage
"The Great Skylight Room"
(Room of Italian Painting)**

**The Winter Palace.
The Golden Reception Room.**
1841. Architect Alexander Briullov

The Hermitage Museum
Leonardo da Vinci. The Litta Madonna.
C. 1490–91

The Hermitage Museum
Jacob Jordaens. The Bean King.
C. 1638

The Hermitage Museum
Rembrandt Harmens van Rijn. Flora.
1634

The Hermitage Museum
Paul Cézanne. Lady in Blue.
C. 1899

The Hermitage Museum
***Henri Rousseau. The Luxembourg
Garden. Monument to Chopin.***
1909

Palace Square
The Alexander Column.
1830–34. Architect Auguste Montferrand
The General Staff building.
1820–28. Architect Carlo Rossi, sculptors
Stepan Pimenov and Vasily Demuth-Malinovsky

The Alexander Column.
Angel with a Cross.
1834. Sculptor Boris Orlovsky

The two-page illustration:

The New Hermitage.
The portico with atlantes.
1848. Architect Leo von Klenze,
sculptor Alexander Terebenev

The Hermitage Theatre.
1783–87. Architect Giacomo Quarenghi

**The Hermitage Theatre
The Auditorium**

The Winter Canal.
1717–19.
**The arch-passage
to the Hermitage Theatre.**
1783–85. Architect Yury Velten

The Marble Palace. The northern front

The Marble Palace. The Marble Hall.
Architect Antonio Rinaldi,
sculptors Mikhail Kozlovsky, Fedot Shubin and A. Valli

The Marble Palace. *1768–85. Architect Antonio Rinaldi, sculptor Fedot Shubin*
Monument to Alexander III. *1906–09. Sculptor Paolo Trubetskoi*

**The raised Troitsky (Kirov) Bridge
with a view of the Peter and Paul
Fortress.**
1903. Architects V. Chabrole and R. Patouliard

**Suvorov Square. Allegorical
monument to Alexander Suvorov.**
*1799 – 1801. Sculptors Mikhail Kozlovsky
and Fiodor Gordeyev (bas-relief),
architect Andrei Voronikhin*

Palace Embankment
The railing of the Summer Gardens.
*1773–84. Architects Yury Velten
and Piotr Yegorov*

The Summer Gardens
The Coffee House.
1826. Architect Carlo Rossi

The Summer Gardens
The Rossi Avenue

The Summer Gardens
The Summer Palace of Peter the Great.
1710–14. Architects Domenico Trezzini and Georg Johann
Mattarnovi, sculptor and architect Andreas Schlüter

The Summer Palace of Peter the Great
The Throne Room

The Alexander Nevsky Lavra
The Trinity Cathedral.
1776–90. Architect Ivan Starov

The Alexander Nevsky Lavra
The Annunciation Church.
1717–23. Architect Domenico Trezzini

The Alexander Nevsky Lavra
The Trinity Cathedral. The central nave.
Architect Ivan Starov, sculptor Fedot Shubin

The Kushelev-Bezborodko dacha.
1773–77

The Smolny Cathedral (Cathedral of the Resurrection of the Smolny Convent).
1748–62. Architect Bartolomeo Francesco Rastrelli

The Kushelev-Bezborodko dacha. The "fence" of lions

The Smolny (Resurrection) Convent ensemble.
1748–69. Architect Bartolomeo Francesco Rastrelli

"I see the capital of the North
Bloom like a flower amongst the rivers"

Gavrila Derzhavin

The masses of stone and masonry flanking the long vistas of St Petersburg's streets and surrounding its semicircular and rectangular squares are separated by the mirror-bands of rivers and canals. In the first half-century of its existence, St Petersburg grew up among dozens of channels, rivers and rivulets. Their number was increased by the digging of canals. The denser building in the city became, however, the less space on its map was occupied by blue veins indicating the natural boundaries of islands and islets.

At the turn of the nineteenth century, the Neva delta (in which St Petersburg is situated) included 48 rivers and canals, washing 101 islands; just under a century later only 42 remained. Nevertheless, the appearance of St Petersburg, which at the same time is an expression of its history and spiritual character, is to a large extent shaped by the Moika and Fontanka Rivers, the Griboyedov (until 1923, Catherine), Kriukov, Swan and Winter Canals.

If the Neva can be said to represent the heroic main theme in St Petersburg's architectural-and-artistic "symphony", then those lesser waterways carry the finer nuances.

For several years Fontanka had no name at all. After 1714, when fountains were installed in the Summer Gardens, the river which supplied them with water finally received a proper name. In the late eighteenth century, all the banks of the Fontanka, which sweeps in a broad arc (6.7 kilometres long) around the central parts of the city, were faced with large granite blocks. Granite landing-stages and decorative metal railings completed the beautification.

The Fontanka is spanned by fifteen bridges. Among them are the celebrated Anichkov Bridge with its four Horse-Tamer sculptures and two former drawbridges with towers.

The banks of the Fontanka were emphatically straightened by the architect Alexei Kvasov, who created the granite-faced landing-stages and the system of squares at the ends of bridges.

The Moika originally flowed from a peat bog close to the Field of Mars. It followed an almost five-kilometre course with many bends, linked to the main course of the Neva by the Fontanka and the Swan Canal. In 1711 the Moika was connected to the Fontanka at its start. Between 1798 and 1811, its banks were faced with granite topped by decorative railings. Fourteen bridges have been constructed across the river.

In contrast to the regular geometric lines given to the Fontanka, the Moika and the Kriukov Canal, for a considerable part of its five-kilometre length the banks of the Griboyedov Canal retain the natural bends of the Krivushi, the small river which formerly flowed across the area. Between 1764 and the 1790s the banks of the canal were decorated with granite and cast-iron railings. The canal is crossed and adorned by twenty-one bridges. Among them are the highly distinctive Lion and Bank Bridges which have become symbols of St Petersburg.

The Griboyedov Canal gains a magical charm from its many twists and turns, which open new, unexpected views, all imbued with a dream-like fascination.

The Mikhailovsky (Engineers') Castle. Northern front.
1797–1800. Architects Vasily Bazhenov and Vincenzo Brenna

The two-page illustration:

The Mikhailovsky (Engineers') Castle
and the adjoining Field of Mars

Monument to Peter the Great in front of the
Mikhailovsky (Engineers') Castle.
1743–47. Carlo Bartolomeo Rastrelli; pediment.
1800. Architect Fiodor Volkov, sculptors Vasily
Demuth-Malinovsky and Pierre Louis Agie

The Sheremetev Palace.
1750–55. Architects Savva Chevakinsky and Fiodor Argunov

The coat-of-arms of the Sheremetev family
Detail of the railing of the Sheremetev Palace.
1837–40. Architect I. Corsini

The Shuvalov Palace.
The Blue Drawing Room.
Arcitect I. Buttatz

The Shuvalov Palace.
*1844–46. Architects Bernard Simon
and Nikolai Yefimov*

The two-page illustration:

The Anichkov Bridge.
*1839–41. Engineer Andrei Gotman,
architect Karl Friedrich Schinkel,
sculptor Piotr Klodt*

The Beloselsky-Belozersky Palace.
*1846–48. Architect Andrei Stakenschneider,
sculptor David Jensen*

**The Beloselsky-Belozersky Palace.
The Golden Reception Room**

The Anichkov Bridge
Sculptural group: Taming a Horse.
1846–50. Sculptor Piotr Klodt

Monument to Catherine the Great.
1862–73. Designed by Mikhail Mikeshin;
sculptors Matvei Chizhov and Alexander Opekushi
architects David Grimm and Victor Schröter

**The Alexandrinsky Theatre
(the Pushkin Academic Drama Theatre).**
*1828–32. Architect Carlo Rossi, sculptors Vasily
Demuth-Malinovsky and Stepan Pimenov*

The Chernyshev (Lomonosov) Bridge.
1785–87.
Obelisks with lanterns.
1915. Architect Ivan Fomin

The Trinity Cathedral of the Life-Guards
of the Izmailovsky Regiment.
1828–35. Architect Vasily Stasov

The St Nicholas-Epiphany Naval Cathedral.
1753–62. Architect Savva Chevakinsky

The St Nicholas-Epiphany Cathedral
The Epiphany (Upper) Church
The iconostasis of the central nave.
Architect Savva Chevakinsky,
 painter Mina Kolokolnikov

The St Nicholas-Epiphany Cathedral
Icon: St Nicholas the Miracle-Worker

The St Nicholas-Epiphany Cathedral
Icon: The Virgin of All Sorrows

The St Nicholas-Epiphany Cathedral
Miracle-working icon:
The Three-Handed Virgin

**The Griboyedov
(Catherine) Canal.**
1764–90
The Kokushkin Bridge.
*1947. Engineer B. Levin;
architect L. Noskov*

**The Griboyedov Canal
The Podyachesky Bridge.**
*1972. Engineer L. Sobolev,
architect L. Noskov*

**The Griboyedov Canal
The Lion Bridge.**
*1825–26. Engineers Georges Tretteur,
sculptor Pavel Sokolov*

The Kazan Cathedral (Cathedral of the Icon of Our Lady of Kazan)
1801–11. Architect Andrei Voronikhin

The Griboyedov Canal. The Bank Bridge.
1825–26. Engineer Georges Tretteur

The Singer Company Building.
1902–04. Architect Pavel Siuzor, sculptors A. Ober and A. Adamson

The Church of the Resurrection
Mosaic: The Entombment.
1887–1900. Artist V. Beliayev

The Church of the Resurrection. Mosaic:
St Prince Vladimir and St Princess Olga.
1887–1900. Artist N. Shakhovskoi

The Church of the Resurrection
(the "Saviour-on-the-Spilt-Blood").
1883–1907. Architect Alfred Parland,
Archimandrite Ignaty (Malyshev)

The Mikhailovsky Garden. Pavilion with a landing-stage.
1825. Architect Carlo Rossi

The Mikhailovsky Palace (Russian Museum)
The northern front.
1819–25. Architect Carlo Rossi

The Mikhailovsky Garden railing
The southern front.
1819–25. Architect Carlo Rossi

The Russian Museum
Icon: St Boris and Gleb.
Mid-15th century. Moscow School

The Russian Museum
Icon: Sts John the Evangelist
and Procopius
16th century. Moscow School

The Russian Museum
Icon: St Demetrius of Thessaloniki.
15th century. Pskov School

The Russian Museum
Icon: Archangel Gabriel (The Angel with the Golden Hair).
12th century

The Russian Museum
The Rokotov Room. Venus.
1792. Sculptor Feodosy Shchedrin

The Russian Museum
The White Hall.
Architect Carlo Rossi, decorators Antonio Vighi,
Barnaba Medici, Giovanni Battista Scotti
and Pietro Scotti

The Russian Museum
Russian Scaevola.
1813. Vasily Demuth-Malinovsky

The Russian Museum
Faun and Bacchante.
1837. Boris Orlovsky

The Russian Museum
The Beginning of Music.
1825. S. Goldberg

The Russian Museum
Alexander Ivanov. The Appearance of Christ to the People.
1836–55

The Russian Museum
Karl Briullov. The Last Day of Pompeii.
1833

The Russian Museum
Vasily Surikov. The Taking of the Snow Fortress.
1891

The Russian Museum
Ilya Repin. The Zaporozhye Cossacks Writing a Mocking Letter to the Turkish Sultan.
1878–91

The Capella.
1887–89. Architect Leonty Benois

Moika Embankment. The Volkonsky House
The Pushkin Memorial Flat

The Moika River
View of the Theatre and Little Koniushenny Bridge.
1829. Engineers Yegor Adam and Georges Tretteur

Moika Embankment. "The Round Market".
1785–90. Architect Giacomo Quarenghi

The Stroganov Palace. The Picture Gallery

The Stroganov Palace.
1752–54. Architect Bartolomeo Francesco Rastrelli

The Mariinsky Palace (Palace of Grand Duchess Maria Nikolayevna).
1839–44. Architect Andrei Stakenschneider

The Mariinsky Palace
The Reception Room

The Mariinsky Palace
The Rotunda

The two-page illustration:

St Isaac's Square
Monument to Nicholas I
1856–59. Sculptors Piotr Klodt, Robert Zaleman, Nikolai Ramazanov, architect Auguste Montferrand

The Yusupov Palace.
1760s. Architect Jean-Baptiste Vallin de la Mothe;
1830–38. Architect Alexander Mikhailov the Younger.
1858–59. Architect Ippolito Monighetti

**The Yusupov Palace
The Moorish Study.**
Architects Ippolito Monighetti and A. Stepanov

**The Yusupov Palace
The Auditorium.**
Architects Ippolito Monighetti and A. Stepanov, artist E. Liphardt

**The Mariinsky Theatre
(the Kirov Opera and Ballet).**
*1859–60. Architect Albert Cavos;
1880. Architect Victor Schröter*

**The Mariinsky Theatre
A scene from the opera "Boris Godunov"**

The Mariinsky Theatre
A scene from the ballet "Swan Lake"

The Mariinsky Theatre
The Auditorium

"New Holland".
*1765–80. Architects Savva Chevakinsky
and Jean-Baptiste Vallin de la Mothe*

**The Large Neva
Admiralty Embankment**

Санкт-Петербург
Альбом
(на английском языке)

Автор вступительной статьи А.Раскин
Художник Д.Трофимов
Редактор М.Лыженкова
Художественный редактор Н.Кутовой
Ответственный за выпуск Н.Гришина

Издательство «П-2»
ЛР № 062197 от 03.02.93.
Санкт-Петербург, ул. Мира, д. 3
Подписано в печать 15.08.96. Формат 60х90$^1/_8$. Усл.п.л 14
Печать офсетная. Тираж 7000 экз. Зак 3734
Отпечатано в типографии АООТ «Иван Федоров».
191126, Санкт-Петербург, ул. Звенигородская, д. 11